BEGIN AGAIN

SONG BOOK

Words and Music by:
Julia A. Royston

Scored by Stephen Key

BK Royston Publishing
P. O. Box 4321
Jeffersonville, IN 47131
502-802-5385
http://www.bkroystonpublishing.com
bkroystonpublishing@gmail.com

© Copyright – 2019

All Rights Reserved. No part of this book may be reproduced, stored in a retrieval system, or transmitted by any means without the written permission of the author.

Cover Design: Jonathan Snorten

ISBN-13: 978-1-946111-74-6

Printed in the United States of America

DEDICATION

I dedicate this music book to anyone who has ever had something happen in your life that made you start all over again. Know that you may be delayed but destiny is still in front of you and you will get there. God's promises are true and absolute. Let this music guide you and console you as you travel this journey called life.

Just Begin Again…

ACKNOWLEDGEMENTS

First, I acknowledge my Lord and Savior Jesus Christ for giving me all of my gifts and especially my gift to write His words.

My husband who is always supportive, loving and encouraging me to utilize all of my gifts and talents. Thank you honey.

To my mother, Dr. Daisy Foree, who is my number one cheerleader and always tells me, "hang in there, you can do it." To my father, Dr. Jack Foree, who is never far away from me in spirit or my heart. I only have to look in the mirror each day to see him.

To Rev. Claude and Mrs. Lillie Royston who support me in everything I do.

Thank you, Stephen Key for being the scribe and musical gift to score all of this music. I am eternally grateful to you and your skillful gift.

To My Louisville Gospel Choral Union Chapter, Mid-West Region and NCGCC family for embracing, encouraging and enabling me to be a better singer, psalmist and teacher. Thank you.

To the rest of my family, I love you and thank you for your prayers, support and love.

INTRODUCTION

I am a singer by birth but a songwriter by favor. God sings the words and the music down into my head and I must grab my phone to record what I hear in my head, pen and/or paper to quickly to get it down. I give God all glory and honor for the favor that He has placed on my life to write songs. I didn't ask for this but He gave it to me so I must dedicate the songs to Him and bless the people with the music. I always tell God, "If You don't give it to me, I don't have it all." To God Be the Glory..

Julia..

FRONTLINE WORSHIPPER

Frontline Worshiper

Words & Music by:
JULIA ROYSTON

© 2014 [INSERT PUBLISHING CO]. All Rights Reserved.
Transcribed by StepKey Music ** info@StepKeyMusic.com

GREAT NEED, GREAT GOD

Great Need, Great God

Words & Music by:
JULIA A. ROYSTON

© 2011 Ju Ju 4ee Publishing (ASCAP) (502-802-5385). All Rights Reserved.
Transcribed by StepKey Music ** (301) 352-3923 ** info@StepKeyMusic.com

IT'S TIME TO PRAISE THE LORD

It's Time to Praise the Lord

Words & Music by:
JULIA A. ROYSTON

♩ = 120

It's time to praise the Lord.

It's time for one ac-cord.

© 2011 JuJu 4ee Publishing LLC, P. O. Box 4321, Jeffersonville, IN 47131 (ASCAP). All Rights Reserved.
*Transcribed by StepKey Music ** info@StepKeyMusic.com*

NOW UNTO HIM

TEACH ME

Teach Me

Words & Music by:
JULIA ROYSTON

© 2010 JuJu4ee Publishing. All Rights Reserved.
Transcribed by StepKey Music ** (301) 352-3923 ** info@StepKeyMusic.com

www.ingramcontent.com/pod-product-compliance
Lightning Source LLC
Chambersburg PA
CBHW042015150426
43196CB00003B/56